Love Prayers

from

RUMI
& Other Sufi Mystics

Copyright © 2018 by Anamchara Books, a division of Harding House Publishing Service, Inc. No part of this book may be reproduced or transmitted in any form or by any means, electronic or mechanical, including photocopying, recording, taping, or any information storage and retrieval system, without permission from the publisher.

9 8 7 6 5 4 3 2 1

ANAMCHARA BOOKS
Vestal, NY 13850
www.AnamcharaBooks.com

IngramSpark paperback ISBN: 978-1-62524-795-7
ebook ISBN: 978-1-62524-496-3

The original poems included in this volume were written centuries ago, mostly in Persian. What you will read here is our modernized English paraphrase of these passionate love prayers to God.

Design by Micaela Grace.

Love Prayers

from
RUMI
& Other Sufi Mystics

DEVON HOLCOMBE,
editor

Love Prayers

from
RUMI
& Other Sufi Mystics

DEVON HOLCOMBE,
editor

Contents

INTRODUCTION ... 7

1. Love Prayers from Rumi ... 9
2. Love Prayers from Hafız ... 87
3. Love Prayers from Rabi'a al-'Adawiyya ... 173
4. Love Prayers from Abu Sa'id ibn Ab'il Khair ... 191
5. Love Prayers from Khajah Abdullah Ansari ... 207
6. Love Prayers from Sanai ... 215
7. Love Prayers from Attar ... 227
8. Love Prayers from Sa'di ... 237
9. Love Prayers from Mahmud Shabistari ... 243
10. Love Prayers from Yunus Emre ... 249
11. Love Prayers from Jami ... 257

Introduction

The Sufis have a unique understanding of God. They are sometimes called the "mystics of Islam," but they themselves would say that they have stepped out beyond any religious category. Their only religion is love—and God is the Beloved who is everything and nothing, all that we can perceive and all that we cannot.

This ancient mystical tradition (its roots lie deep in the first millennium of the Common Era) teaches that God is always within us—even when we feel very far from God. We cannot escape from God, for God is like the air we breathe, present everywhere, within us and without. All things, good and bad, are aspects of the God who loves us. When we enter into a love relationship with this Divine Beloved, we love God in every person, every place, every creature.

The prayers in this book were inspired by the work of Sufi poets who lived a thousand or so years ago—and yet their earthy, crude, ecstatic, and passionate poetry speaks to us in the twenty-first century as powerfully as ever. No matter how we label ourselves religiously, our spiritual lives will be enriched if we can pray as they did—as though we were head over heels in love with God.

1
Love Prayers from Rumi

JALĀL AD-DĪN MUHAMMAD RŪMĪ MAWLĀNĀ, better known as simply Rumi, was born in Persia (modern-day Iran) in 1207. He was a Sufi mystic and a prolific and inspired writer. After writing many other shorter works, he spent the last twelve years of his life writing a single poem, the Masnavi (*Rhyming Couplets of Profound Spiritual Meaning*), which is thousands of lines long.

Rumi's influence spread far beyond Persia—and far past his own lifetime. Through the centuries, his words enriched the spiritual lives of Muslims, and today, people from all religions find inspiration and wisdom in Rumi's writing. His words have been translated into many languages, even as they continue to be read in Persian in Iran, Afghanistan, and other Persian-speaking nations. Meanwhile, he has become America's best-selling poet.

Like all Sufis, Rumi had an intense and passionate relationship with God. In his poetry, Rumi also often refers to Jesus. As Muslims, the Sufis used different language from Christians to describe Jesus' spiritual role, and they focused on different aspects of his life. They believed that Jesus was both a messenger from God and a perfect model of the love relationship that's possible between God and human beings. Many of Rumi's poems also reveal an even deeper meaning to be found in Jesus. "In the fire of the Divine love," Rumi wrote, "I saw an entire universe, and Jesus breathed through each and every particle."

Move me,
Beloved God,
beyond the tangle of my worries.
Teach me to silence my noisy heart.
May I flow down
and down
and down
in ever-widening circles
of Being.

When my mind tells me
there's no possible way ahead,
Beloved,
may Love whisper to me,
"Yes, there is a way!
I've gone that way
a thousand times before."
When my mind says,
"Danger lies ahead.
It will hurt too much,
if I surrender all,"
let me hear Love's laughter,
as I hear Love say,
"The pain is only in your mind."
Teach me to find the roses
hidden in my pain,
so that I may discover
within my inner self,
rose garden
after rose garden.

Jesus, change my brass
to gold,
Take the gold that's already
within my heart
and turn it into pearls.
And if You find any pearls
already in my heart,
make them more beautiful
than the moon.

When I question
the reality of Your Love,
remind me to look
in the same place in my heart
from which the question springs.

I'm selling all my intelligence
and my skills
on eBay, Beloved One.
I'll use the money
to buy wonder.

Beloved,
I realize now:
when I keep shouting,
"Further on!
I must reach a distant goal!"
I've cut myself off
from "here."
I'm living in a fantasy
about the future
while I miss the present moment.
When I run back and forth,
looking for a road
that leads to future success,
I miss the path
that leads me to my Self.

You promise me,
Beloved God,
that You are here with me,
within my very being.
And yet I can only understand You
so slowly, never completely,
always indirectly.
When I find enlightenment at last,
I'll say, "Why here You are,
right where You've always been,
within my heart!
How could I have been so blind?"
But if I had always seen You here
inside me,
I would have never searched
for You.
The long journey toward You,
is the only way I come to know
Your presence.

The wine bottle of Your grace
is never empty.
If I don't have enough,
it's only the fault of my wine glass.
You are like moonlight
that fills the entire sky.
How much the moonlight
fills my room
depends on the size
of my windows.

Since my life is the cup
that holds Your wine, Beloved,
remind me to treat it with respect.
Since Love designed me
to hold You within me,
let me not forget
my true dignity.

My work, God,
is to surrender my head
to the guillotine
of life.
Your job
is to give me
a new head.

Meet me, Beloved,
in the grassy field
that lies beyond all my ideas
about right and wrong.
I'll lie on my back with You
and look at the sky.

The minute I heard
my first love story,
I started searching for You,
Divine Lover.
I didn't realize
You were in me
all along.
I don't have to seek for You.
I simply have to seek
the barriers within my inner self
that hide You from my sight.

If every little friction
gets me upset,
Beloved,
how will the mirror of my heart
ever be polished?

When I was born,
Beloved,
You gave me wings.
So why do I keep
crawling through life
like a worm?

"Knock," You say to me,
"and I'll open My door and ask you in.
Disappear,
so you no longer see your own ego,
and I'll make you shine
like the sun.
Stumble and fall,
and I'll lift you up to heaven.
Become nothing,
and I'll make you everything."

Help me, Beloved,
to ignore the voices that tell me worry
and sadness are what I should be feeling.
They're just pushing me
backward.

Your only language,
Loving Friend,
is silence.
Everything else
is only
a poor translation.

Make me grateful, Beloved,
for whatever comes my way.
Remind me that it's all
a message from You.

There's a candle in my heart,
Beloved,
just waiting to be lit.
There's an emptiness within me
just waiting to be filled.

Remind me, Beloved,
that when everything
seems ruined,
treasure is found in shipwrecks.

Yesterday,
Beloved One,
I thought I was so smart
that I could change the world.
Today,
I'm wise enough to know
I can only change myself.

Help me, God,
to sing like a bird,
not wanting to impress anyone,
not caring what people think
but simply because
I was made to sing.

Today,
my heart's Beloved,
I woke up scared and empty.
I could have gone to work,
but instead I picked up my guitar
Let my work be
the beauty I love most,
There are hundreds of ways
to kiss Life's lips.

My inner self
is a guest house,
and every morning
a new guest arrives.
Sometimes it's joy,
other days it's sadness.
Some days irritation and aggravation;
other days a new insight
arrives like an unexpected visitor.
Help me, Divine Lover,
to welcome each and every guest.
Even if a crowd of sorrows
comes pushing through my door
and robs all my furniture,
give me strength
to treat them like honored guests.

How do I know?
The guests I thought were thieves
may actually be making space
for something new
and wonderful.
So when painful feelings
come knocking on my door,
help me, God,
to greet them with laughter
and invite them in.

Help me, Beloved,
to stop serving my friends
meals of my complaints.
Remind me that they hunger
for happiness, not pain.
Untie my wings.
Strip all jealousy from my soul.
Let me fly like a bird,
carrying everyone around me
into the sky.

I've failed You so many times,
Beloved One,
and yet You say to me,
"Come, wanderer, join my caravan.
Come, even though you have broken
a thousand promises.
This is no caravan of despair and failure.
We'll cross the desert together,
dancing with joy."

Set me on fire, Beloved.
And then remind me
to spend my time
with people
who fan the flames.

Help me not to grieve,
Beloved One.
Remind me
that all will be returned to me
in another form.

Why am I so afraid of death,
Beloved?
When I died as mineral,
I became a plant.
When I died as a plant,
I rose up as an animal.
I died as animal,
and now I am a human being.
When did dying
make me any less?

I've been walking along
the edge of the ocean,
my pants rolled up
to keep them dry.
Now I'm ready
to strip off all my clothes
and dive naked into You.
I want to go beneath the surface,
deeper and deeper,
a thousand times deeper!

When I look out
at my garden in winter,
Loving Friend,
remind me
that even though it looks quiet,
even dead,
the roots are dancing,
having a party
beneath the ground.

You keep turning me
back and forth, God,
from one feeling to another.
Are You using these opposites
so that I'll have two wings,
instead of only one?

I always thought that I was me.
Now I find out I was You
and never knew it
until now.

Why don't You answer me,
Beloved God,
when I pray?
Why do I get nowhere
in my spiritual life?
Why don't You help me?
And then Your answer
comes to me:
"I was the One
who called your heart to prayer.
I was the One
who made you long for Me.
Your longing
was My message to you.
Your voice calling out,
'God, God, God!'
was Me saying,
'Here I am.'

All your frustration,
your sense of helplessness,
your yearning for something more,
all that was My voice speaking to you.
I was the magnet for your prayers,
and I am the One who made them fly."

Make me like plowed earth, Beloved,
moist soil where flowers will grow.
Remind me that nothing
grows on sharp rocks.

Help me not to get upset
if my cup is dirty.
So long as it holds Your wine,
why should I care?
When the wine is good,
who worries about the wine glass?

I've opened my window,
Divine Lover.
Come to me in the moonlight,
and press Your face against mine.
Breathe into me.
I'm closing
the speech-door of my bedroom
and I've opened up the love-window.
I know moonlight
won't come in the door,
only through the window.

What is my body, God?
It's only a shadow
of a shadow of Your love,
and yet somehow,
it contains the entire universe.

My mind is bursting, Beloved,
filled with the joy of discovery.
My heart is expanding,
larger than it's ever been before.
Every cell of my body
has taken wing
and flies through the universe,
each one seeking
Your countless faces.

Make this wound in my heart,
Beloved,
an opening
where Your Light
can enter me.

Beloved,
I sense within me
a morning
that's simply biding its time,
waiting to burst open
into Light.

At the very moment,
when my legs were too heavy
to walk another step,
You gave me wings.
Astonished,
I felt them spread
and lift me high
into the air.

Kill my ego, God,
the empty, troublemaking
version of myself.
Burn away the darkness
of my false self
and then my true Self
will shine like sunlight.
Dissolve my ego
into the Being
who is everything.

I am filled with You.
Mere existence is a dance of joy.
Skin, blood, and bone,
brain and soul,
You fill me completely.
There's no room in me now
for either doubt or belief.
None of that matters anymore.
My life is only
Your life.

Christ is everyone
in the entire world
and every thing as well.
When I remember that,
Beloved Friend,
there's no room in me
for hypocrisy or dogma.
Why would I offer people sour soup
when such sweet water
is free for the taking
everywhere?

The miracle of Jesus
is simply himself, his Being.
Help me, God,
to forget everything else—
dogma and creed,
heresy and division—
and simply fall down
and worship.

I'm not equipped to seek You,
but I'll trust that no equipment
is necessary
on the road to You.
When people ask me
what I have accomplished in life,
I'll have to tell them, Beloved,
"Only Love."

Remind me, Loving One,
that every person
has their own unique path
to You,
and yet all paths are the same:
they all lead to You.
No matter what religion we follow—
or don't follow—
we all praise One Being.
May all our voices,
from our many ways of believing,
rise together,
singing a single love song
to You.

I am a fish, God,
and You are the ocean.
I can't live on dry land
away from You.

When Your image,
Beloved Friend,
burns away my selfish thoughts,
then my mind, my entire life
flows into contemplation,
and I find Union
with You.
Now, in the middle of my house,
is a garden full of flowers.
When I fall asleep,
the stars are my blankets,
and I lie so close to You
that Your hair mingles
with mine.
Your reflection flames out
and the entire Earth
becomes silk and velvet.

When I write Your Name in the dust,
each grain of sand
becomes an angel.
Why should I speak,
when even Nothingness
says Your Name?
The smallest thought
about Your Love
is weighty,
like a dense kernel.
When I see Love,
everything I thought I knew
falls down in a faint.
I'll keep silent now,
while the entire world dissolves
and there is only You.

Beloved,
make me
like melting snow,
so that I can wash away myself
from myself.

Why am I so enchanted
with the external world,
Beloved,
when a deep mine of gold
lies within me?

Love," whispers my Friend.
"And then die.
Your real life begins on the other side.
Become the sky,
wide open to both Earth
and Heaven.
Take a sledge hammer to the walls
you've built around your heart.
Escape.
Walk out and be stunned,
like a blind person
who can suddenly see.
You're surrounded by smog,
but if you die,
you'll slip free
out into the clear air
where you can see the Light.

Be quiet.
Your old life was so busy
because you were always
trying to run away from Silence.
Look at the moon.
It shines in silence.
So can you.
Don't procrastinate.
Do it now.
I'm waiting just for you."

Beloved God,
I've been sitting here in prison
while all the while,
I've held the key in my hand.
I've been covered in dust
when I'm standing
right next to a clear waterfall.
The very fact that I desire
something else
proves that there IS
something else.
Wandering
without knowing where I'm going
gives me a map to follow.
A secret freedom
shines through a crevice
I can only glimpse.

Each plant stem and tree trunk
standing stiff and rigid,
separate from one another,
connects with agile roots
that intertwine beneath the ground.
But why do I say all these things?
When I'm with You,
my Heart's Lover,
I don't need to speak.
Love fills the silence.

Make me certain,
Beloved,
of only two things:
first, that whatever I believe now
will turn out to be mistaken,
and second, that there is always
new wisdom to learn.
Remind me
that asking
is the most important half
of knowing.

If I don't fulfill
Your purpose for me—
the inner purpose of my soul—
I might as well be using a golden chalice
for cooking turnips.

I have many interests
and many skills,
but they are all branches
from the single root of my being:
You, Beloved God.

Many things come and go.
My thoughts,
my emotions,
my opinions,
my dreams and fantasies.
Only You remain the same.

Teach me not to worry
quite so much, Beloved Friend,
about my body's pains.
Remind me that my body
is only a suit of clothes.
When I'm with my lover,
I like the way he looks in his clothes,
but I don't shower kisses
on his jeans and T-shirt.
Why then should I care so much
about my soul's clothing?
I have other hands and feet
besides the ones I see.
I have a spirit body,
so why should I dread
setting aside my visible flesh?

I am only breath now, Beloved.
I am not a Christian,
not a Jew,
not a Hindu,
not a Muslim,
not a Buddhist.
I don't identify myself
with any nation or group of people.
I claim no religious story as my own.
I am only Yours,
the breath that breathes me.

I am like a flute
and You are the breath
that makes music from me.
I am like a mountain
and You are the echo that rings from my rocks.
I am like a chess piece,
preoccupied with the business
of victory and defeat,
but all victories and all defeats
come from You, Lovely One.
Soul of my soul,
why do I exist
when only You are Being?
My existence is really nonexistence,
but You, Absolute Being,
manifest Yourself in me,
mortal though I am.

The wind that blows me forward
is Your gift.
I exist because You
bring me into Being.

For years, I worked so hard,
trying to tug my own existence
out of emptiness.
Then, with a single wave of Your hand,
You put an end
to my pointless, never-ending work.
Now I am free.

If you listen,
you'll hear the call of Love
ringing out through each moment of time
in every thing you see and touch.

We are going to the sky—
do you want to come along?
We have lived in Heaven;
we have been friends with angels;
and now we are going back,
for Heaven is our home.
The Highest High is our only goal,
and the day of our death
is our wedding day with Eternity.
That's the day we will finally
be One.

"You are too harsh with me,"
I complain to my Beloved.
My Beloved answers,
"You came into My Presence
shouting out, 'Here am I!
Look at me!'
So I gave you a knock on the head,
to wake you up,
for this is a sacred place, not a barnyard.
This is the sanctuary where Love lives.
Rub the sleep from your eyes,
and you'll see what I mean.
Take a good look,
and you'll see your true Self,
not that make-believe thing
you tried to show Me."

The world brims over
with intoxication.
Every object, every creature,
is a wine bottle of delight.
But don't gulp it all down at once.
Be a wine connoisseur
who tastes with care
so that her palate is not dulled.
Choose the wines
that are pure, free from fear.
Choose the wine
that never ever says,
"You should do this,"
"You're supposed to do that,"
"You ought to be this."

Drink the wine
that fills you with the kind of energy
a horse has when he's been untied
and is simply wandering around,
enjoying the sun and the grass.

When we listen
to guitars and trumpets,
trombones and banjos,
ukuleles and pianos,
their music echoes
the same Song the stars sing.
We sense the Truth
that is always the melody,
weaving through every sound.
After all, we share DNA with the first humans;
we heard with them the songs of angels.
Our memory may be dulled with sadness,
but still, the echo of that Song
sounds in our ears.
Music nourishes love.
Music lifts our souls into a higher realm.

Music blows on the ashes in our hearts,
and makes the sparks hidden there
glow brighter.
Listen to the music!
Be fed with joy and peace.

2

Love Prayers
from Hafiz

HAFIZ was a Sufi who lived in Iran sometime in the fourteenth century. He was a mystic—but his experience of God was very down to earth. He wasn't afraid to use metaphors for God that he drew from daily life—everything from the weather to work, from human interactions to drinking wine, from nature to sex. He wrote of ecstatic joy, but he also wrote of sorrow and anxiety, boredom and fear. A prolific poet, Hafiz wrote as many as five thousand poems (though many of them have been lost). His endless stream of inspiration grew deeper and more intense the older he got.

No matter how we label ourselves religiously, our spiritual lives will be enriched if we can pray as Hafiz did—as though we were madly in love with God.

Beloved,
remind me never to say to the world:
"You owe me."
May I be like the Sun,
which simply shines its light on the Earth,
down through the millennia,
never asking for anything in return.
May I shine love on the world,
unconditionally,
no matter what.

Your love, Beloved,
will someday split me
open.

You sliced off
pieces of Your own soul, Beloved,
and then wove them into a blanket
to wrap around my heart.

Beloved,
remind me to run away
from anything
that doesn't strengthen
my budding wings.

Beloved,
put the full moon in each of my eyes,
so that my eyes will always say,
in sweet moon language,
what every other eye
in this world
is dying to hear.

You know how I am, Beloved,
when I haven't been drinking from Your love.
My face is tight,
my muscles cramp.
The look in my eyes worries little children.
When I look in the mirror,
that look worries me too!
I even scare the angels,
with this insanity of mine
that sets myself up as though
the entire world were my enemy,
even myself.
Oh, Beloved, You know the way I get,
when I haven't drunk enough of Your love.
I criticize everything my friends say.
I weigh every word they speak,
as though they were
a bunch of dead fish on a scale.

I pull out a ruler to measure
every angle of those I love,
when they should never be measured,
only loved and trusted.
You know the way I get, Beloved,
when I haven't drunk from Love's hands.
That's why all the wise teachers
talk about the vital need
to keep coming back to You, God.
Then I will get to know You.
I'll see how playful You are,
how You are always there,
longing, yearning to lend me a hand.
You tell me to bring my cup to You,
because the only thing You want to do,
is quench my thirst for freedom.
And then,
when I am sane again,
the only thing I'll care about
is giving love.

Beloved One,
love is the funeral pyre
where I have lain my living body.
All my false ideas about myself,
the ego that has given me such pain
and caused me such anxiety,
has burned to ash,
the closer I've come
to You.

The same Beloved One who shines
so jubilantly from the angels' eyes,
who screams from the very guts
of everlasting life—
You are shining also
through all my tangled knots,
from the web of thought and muscles
that makes me who I think I am.

Today, Beloved,
I'm going to makes myself a home
with the birds.
I'm going to listen to music all day,
and for just one day,
I refuse to talk about anything
that's upsetting.
I'll open up my eyes,
and see only You.
And then, finally, I'll have
a little peace.

Beloved, I want to hear Your Words.
What lies at the root of every word You speak?
Only one thing—love.
But it's a love so deep,
so sweet,
it could only express itself
with scent and sound and color.
It had to create an entire world
to tell me how much
You love me.

What is destiny, Beloved?
Is it written on the gate of heaven?
I think it's a sign that says,
"Destiny brought you here,
to this very moment
(as you sit here reading these words)—
and it's all part of your ticket home.
Everything, absolutely everything,
brings you back to God."

I see You everywhere, God.
But I'm keeping it a secret.

The fish never gets back to the sea,
until he says,
"There's just something not right
about me riding in my Subaru,
when I'm feeling so damned thirsty."
And THAT'S the first step home.

The world has been dropping
gravel on my face,
instead of snow.
It hurts.
Can I come in, Beloved,
out of the storm?

Beloved,
I lift my glass in a toast,
to every soul on Earth.
"Here's to you!" I say.
"Because you've been so brave."

I quit, Beloved.
I've become skilled
at my own personal form of insanity,
but it's hard work,
bringing so much pain to myself.
So now I'm going to retire.

Beloved, show me Your mirror,
as clear as a mountain lake,
so that I can see
the beautiful, ancient warrior,
and the sacred life that fills the universe—
all the pieces of You
that I carry inside me.

There's nothing under my feet now.
I've surrendered it all to You,
my Beloved One.
Now I'm like a singing air creature.
And I feel the rose inside me
opening and opening
and opening.

When I was young,
I knew You, God
as all children do.
But not the God the grown-ups knew,
the God of don'ts
and big words I didn't understand.
The God I knew then
said only four words to me,
over and over:
"Come dance with Me!
Come dance with Me!"

Beloved One,
I will always lean my heart
as close to You as I can get.

You teach me, God,
that every heart
always gets the thing
it asks for most.

Beloved,
here's the kind of Friend You are:
without any reminders of the past
You slip into my house at night,
and while I am sleeping,
You silently carry off
all my dirty laundry,
in Your beautiful
hands.

You have made my heart
a thousand-stringed instrument
that can only be tuned with Your love.

I hate to make any claims
about the power of prayer.
But this much I know:
whenever I pray
somewhere in this world, Beloved,
You make something good happen.

I'm letting go now, Beloved One,
of all my narrow categories,
my rigid way of looking at others.
Make me loose with compassion,
willing to float, willing to drown
in Your delicious
sea of Love.

Remind me, Beloved God,
that this world is insane.
It's not even exactly real.
So even though I've built a house here,
even though the postal service
delivers letters to my mailbox,
my real address
is somewhere else.

When I'm creating something,
Beloved,
writing a poem, a story, a song,
sometimes it feels like
I just don't have the strength
to wring out another drop
of light.
I'm ready to cry into my beer—
and then the poem, the story, the song,
climbs up on the counter of the bar,
lifts her skirts and winks at me,
and all the light in the sky
falls
just like that
into my mind.

When I refuse to love, Beloved One,
I'm letting go of my safety line.
This mountain I'm climbing
is far too dangerous
for that.

You are a creative Lover
with many positions
for loving,
ten thousand different ways
to embrace me:
each curve of a tree branch,
the world's infinite shapes,
spring's orchestra of scents,
the daily explosion of light
like passionate lips against my skin.
Existence twirls her skirt,
countless universes hidden in the folds.
You feel my every breath,
falling against Your inconceivable,
everywhere-present
Body.

Beloved,
give me courage
to lean out from the dark place
where I've been hiding
and open up my mouth
and my mind,
so that You can pour
pure radiance
into me.

God,
I don't tell all my secrets
even to my lover.
I've counted
the moles on his ass,
but I respect his shyness
and keep the tally to myself.
You and I, though,
we've made vows to each other,
to be even more intimate
than that.

Beloved,
I think I caught something from You
last night when I was
singing under the stars.
I think it was
a happiness virus.

Look, Beloved!
Today's my wedding day,
and the sun is my best man.
He stands there at the front of the church,
whistling,
because I've finally found the courage
to marry forgiveness.
At last, I've found the courage
to marry Love.

Beloved,
You've boiled down all my desires,
and now just two things
are left:
more love
and more happiness.

Wake me up, Beloved,
so that my heart will be like the sky
pouring out light.

I need love, Beloved,
because love is life.
It's creation's
greatest joy.

Beloved,
when I'm lying on my deathbed,
I don't want to say
to the world I'm leaving,
"I wish I'd kissed you more."

Beloved One,
worrying is the job that's kept me busy
day and night,
but it hasn't earned me a single cent.
So I quit.
Now I'm checking the want ads.
I'd like a better job.

I'm waiting for the moment, God,
when I finally see human beings
shut down their weapons
right before they deploy them,
because they've finally realized:
we all have just one flesh.

Beloved,
I've been living in this hotel's worst room,
the same room where fear lives.
I've called the hotel desk clerk
to let her know
I'm ready now to move
to a better room.
This time,
I'd like a room with windows.

If the great religions are the ocean liners,
every sane person I know
has jumped overboard.
Now it's time, Beloved One, for the poets
to send out the lifeboats.

Beloved, You know how much
I want to be free of these sad feelings,
this anxiety and worry,
and yet You say to me,
"Don't let it go yet.
Let it cut you still more deeply.
It needs to ferment inside you
a little longer,
because when it does,
it will season you
as no other ingredient can."

I'm looking for You, Beloved,
seeking out Your Presence,
and then I hear You say,
"If you're looking for Me, sweetheart,
why are you hiding your own face?
Before you look everywhere else,
try looking inside."

Beloved One,
I'm wandering through Your wild place,
exploring the untamed land.
Look there!
A lover's song
is making Jesus dance.

I don't need to go on a pilgrimage
to find You, Beloved One.
You are at home
here
within me.

Only You,
Illumined One,
can keep seducing the formless world
to take shape.
Only You could find
my inner self.
The word "two"
makes You laugh out loud.
Only You
could teach me
love.

Help me, Beloved One,
to leave behind the familiar
for just a little while.
Let me stretch out,
as though I'm lying on a bed,
all my senses, all my muscles,
open,
like windows lifted up
to catch the first breezes of spring
blowing off the hills.
When night falls, bring me up
to the rooftop of my house
where I will be like a blooming flower,
filling the friendly world around me
with the scent of joy.

For just one day,
Beloved,
help me to move
into a different room
inside my mind.
If I look out a new set of windows,
who knows what I might see?

Every line of all Your latitudes
circles the equator in my heart,
"Hello!" I shout to all my thousand forms.
I surf the invisible wave
that flows from You
and carries me back home.
All of heaven's latitudes
are sitting around a campfire
talking among themselves,
as they stitch themselves together
into the one Great Circle
that is You,
the same Great Circle
that is in me.

I will drink from You, Beloved,
for You are like
an enormous jug of wine,
filled to the brim with Unity.
Wash from my heart
all the empty sorrows,
the futile worries.
Make my heart
as wide and full
as Your enormous jug of wine.
Why would I want
to keep my heart shut tight,
like an uncorked bottle of wine?
When I drink Your wine,
Beloved,
you wash away my selfishness.
I have no need to boast,
to puff up my ego
and strut around.

Make me like a stone on the ground,
content to be unnoticed,
rather than always trying
to be up in the sky
floating around like a cloud.
Clouds are wet,
but they lack a body.
May the wine I drink from You
connect to my inner self
so that now it has a body
all its own.
Let me cut the neck of hypocrisy,
my self-righteous ego
that's too stiff to drink from You.

I'm an old workhorse, Beloved,
tired and weary,
but I've thrown myself at Your feet.
Give me Your boundless pastures.
May I rest in You forever.

You've taught me so much, God,
that I can no longer call myself
a Christian
or a Hindu
or a Muslim
or a Buddhist
or a Jew.
Beloved Truth,
You have shared
so much of Yourself
with me
that now I don't think of myself
as a man,
a woman,
an angel,
or even a soul.

You have befriended
my inner self,
and Your love has turned to ash
everything I thought I was.
Now I am free
from all my ideas,
all my concepts and images.
I'm empty of everything
but You.

My thoughts are like a lover,
giving me as much joy
as any warm body.
I'm ready, Beloved,
to stop making love with form,
even though it's Your beloved child.
Why should I spend my time with it,
when You Yourself
are standing right next to me
Your arms held out.
Prayer is my lover now.
I've let everything else go.

If You would shine
Your love-light in my heart,
I'd shine brighter than a dozen suns.
I need to wash life's tarnished copper
off my hands, because
I'm ready now to be Love's alchemist,
working only with gold.
I'm done with just thinking about love.
Now I'm taking the leap
into the sea of Your love.
Up until now,
I've only been getting my toes wet,
wetting a single strand of hair.
Now I'm dunking my head under the waves.
I want to see only You
so that my eyes are finally clear.

Beloved,
keep me close to everything
that makes me glad I am alive.

Give me the courage, Beloved,
to let You drag me by the hair,
ripping from my hands
all the toys that bring me no real joy.
Sometimes, Beloved, I know You get tired
of speaking to me sweetly.
You want to rip to shreds
all my ideas about what truth is,
all the ideas that make me fight
within myself and with others,
making the world weep
on days when it should be laughing.
I'll let You lock me in a cell with You,
where I'll be at Your mercy.
You can kick me around,
hold me upside down,
and shake all the nonsense out of me.
This isn't an image of You, God,
that people like to hear!

If they thought You were
in a playful, drunken mood,
they'd pack their bags
and get out of town.
I'm in Your hands, Beloved.
Shake me all You want.
Break all my tidy teacups
so that I'll have no more
religious tea parties
where I sit there making conversation
about You.

Now that I've seen Your Light,
shining in the darkness
like a laughing candle,
I'm ready, my Love,
to give up
the dim life I've been living
inside my head.

Bring me to the point, God,
where my relationship with You
is like this:
I bump into You somewhere—
doesn't really matter where,
it could be a forest path
or a city street—
and this time, You and I
won't go on our separate ways.
You'll climb into my pocket.
I'll take You along with me
because You are me.

Remind us,
Beloved God,
that we humans are
house-sitting for You
here on this Earth.
Remind us
not to forget
to water the plants
and feed the animals.

I'd be silly, Beloved,
to say that You are something separate,
something "out there,"
when all the while,
You're all around me.
It would be like floating in the sea
and insisting
that there's no water touching me,
that water is not pressing gently
against every inch of my skin.

The sun won a beauty contest,
and now it's a jewel on Your finger.
The Earth settled
for being a toe ring on Your foot.
It's never regretted its decision!
The mountains have grown tired of us
being such a rude audience.
We've fallen sound asleep
and totally missed
their grand performance.
They got tired
of putting on their show
for a snoring crowd,
so they poked me in the eye,
and woke me up.
They gave me a good idea,
and now I'm
like a diamond with wings,
rising into You.

I am like a fish,
Beloved.
I can only survive
in a watery world.
But now I'm exchanging my gills
for lungs and wings.
Now I can fly
higher and higher,
breathing the air of Your love.

You have made me
a guardian of Your beauty.
I protect the Light.
The only reason
I followed You into this world:
was so that I could say
to everyone I meet,
"Laugh! Dance! Love!"
I am Your companion.
I walk each day by Beauty's side.
I guard the Truth.
And every man and woman and child,
every plant and beast,
every stone and drop of water
is a harbinger of Your Joy,
a harbinger of Light.

Give me a poke, Beloved,
when I start to moon at the sky
doing nothing.
Reach Your hand, my Friend,
into my inner being.
Heal my wounded wings,
and then I will unfurl my heart
into You.

Within the rosebud sleeps the rose.
Within the world
Your glory flames:
on barroom floors
and church walls;
where the call to prayer
falls from the muezzin;
where church bells call
the faithful to the Cross of Christ;
and where the shofar sounds
in synagogues.
You are wherever
Love falls
like light upon our faces.

I want to scatter roses at Your feet.
I want to shatter Heaven's roof
and build You a new foundation
here on Earth.
When armies march
to shed Love's blood,
I'll overthrow them
by pouring wine into a glass,
playing a sweet song on my guitar,
and clapping and singing Your song.
Then I'll dance all night
with You, Beloved.

Does depression call your name?
Are you getting invitations
from your old bad habits,
asking you to come back?
Don't listen.
Instead, keep squeezing new light
from the sunshine,
from your work and prayer,
from music and every glance
from the Beloved.
Stop trying to buy life
with counterfeit money.
Sweetheart, if you go back to your old ways,
you'll be like someone
tied to the back end of a farting pig.
Instead, learn what delights
the Beloved.

Those are the things
that will bring you freedom
and life.
Be wise, be sweet.
Don't cast your ballot for depression.
Don't vote for those old habits.
Cast all your votes
for dancing
with the Beloved!

Do you know how beautiful you are?
I don't think you do.
But believe me, sweetheart,
there's a parade that marches
out from you,
carrying a startling, secret song
that only you can teach the world.
You think you're ordinary,
but you can't see what the Beloved sees,
for you are wild, lovely,
full of color and wonder.
Even if you can't see your heart's parade,
others will.
Believe me. You are amazing.
So sing along with your heart,
and I'll join in,
and together we will serenade
the Beloved.

Spending a day in silence
can be like going on a journey.
In the silence, you'll be able to hear
your own soul
singing its song,
beating its rhythms on a drum.
After all, when we talk, most of the time
we're just trying to build up the walls
around the broken fortresses of our hearts.
Surrender to silence.
Yield to light and joy.
Dance within your heart
as you celebrate Love.

Want to hear a secret?
Laughter is simply this—
the sound of God calling,
"Time to get up!"
It is the sun coming out
from behind that cloud
you've been carrying over your head
for way too long.
Laughter is the Light
breaking open the ground
to build the structure
of your real Self.
Laughter is the North Star,
held steady in the sky
by the Beloved One,
who is always saying,
"Yes, sweetheart, come this way.
Come this way!

Come toward Love.
Come toward Me.
Your feet already know the Dance.
Every cell in your body
knows it too.
So come closer to Me."
What is laughter?
It is the song of a soul
waking up.

Standing by the Beloved's side,
reach out to this world.
Offer the comfort
you have drawn from the bottomless lake
of Truth and Love.
Don't turn your back
on the Earth's faltering steps.
The Earth needs you to be her lover,
your mouth open and sweet against her skin.
Make love to her rivers and seas,
to her furred creatures and feathered ones,
to those who gleam with scale and fin,
and to humans who are bleeding,
desperate for the Beloved's touch.
Be the hands of the Divine.
Be an open mouth against your lover's skin.

Every now and then, I suppose,
it could be beneficial to think to yourself,
"I should be doing so much more with my life.
After all, I have so much to offer.
I ought to be doing more."
But only spend a moment with the thought.
The rest of time,
try to see yourself the way God does.
God never gets confused,
the way you do,
with "should" and "ought."
God has no false illusions about your talents,
but the Beloved knows your true nature,
that you and God are One.
Dear one, Venus just whispered in my ear
a secret she wants me to share with you.
She said she's been your mirror
for centuries,
stealing your light so she'll shine.

She knows the truth, though.
She knows that you're the one
who is the Beloved's child,
shining with Divine Light.

We get so confused about our role in life.
We think we're here to win a war.
We think it's us against them,
when all along we are here
to surrender
more and more deeply
to Love.
Sweetheart, run from anything
that could weaken your wings.
Don't listen to anyone
who tries to stab a knife into your awareness
that you are beloved of the Beloved.
I'm not saying you shouldn't be obedient,
but be obedient only to that Voice
that's shouting, "Come out and play with Me."

The Beloved says to me,
"I rain because the fields call for Me.
I weave my Light into words
so that your mind can become
a brighter place.
I wrapped up My laughter like a birthday gift,
and I left it there beside your bed,
where you'd find it in the morning.
I planted my wisdom next to every tree,
I hung My love from every flower.
So go ahead, go a little crazy.
I've given you everything,
and now you too can hang treasures
on every star and tree, every bird and flower.
Listen! I am singing to you
from within your flesh.
Every cell of your body
is reaching out to Me."

You have within you
all the ingredients you need
to whip up a batch
of pure JOY.
So go ahead.
Mix them up!
Stir them all together!
Bake up some joy,
and then share it with the world.

Stop looking for doctrines
and religious certainties.
You have no need of them,
for you are climbing life's ladder
that leads to the Beloved's door.
The only way you can find Love
is by loving.
Love is life. Love is creation. Love is joy.
Love is the ladder that leads
to the Beloved's door.

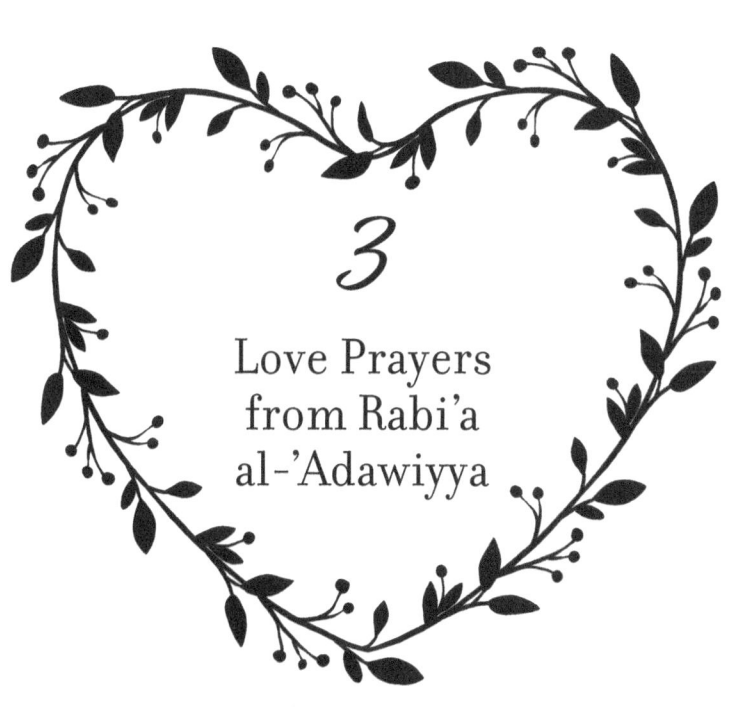

3

Love Prayers from Rabi'a al-'Adawiyya

RABI'A (717–801 CE) was an orphan who as a child was sold as a slave—and in the midst of slavery, fell in love with the God she called Beloved. According to legend, her master set her free when he saw her praying with light shining all around her. After her long life of hardship, she achieved a state of enlightened self-realization. When asked how she discovered the secret, she answered, "You speak of how—but I only know the how-less."

When nothing comes between
You and me,
the only speech I need is longing.
When I taste You,
I know you.
But when I try to explain You,
I end up telling lies.
How can I describe
Something who is like the air I breathe?
How can I draw the outlines
of Someone who fills my entire being?
My very journey through life
is a sign of You.

I have two ways
of loving You, Beloved.
One way is selfish, ego-centered.
The other springs from my true Self.
The selfish love
has plenty of ideas about You.
But the other love
lifts the veil between You and me.
Now I feast my eyes
on Your Living Face.

I can't blame
my loneliness and depression
on the outside world.
It springs from deep within
my inner being.
No psychologist can cure it.
No doctor can give me a pill
to make me feel better.
Only union with You,
my Friend,
will heal me.

You, Beloved,
are my heart's companion.
But my body
is quite happy to hang out
with human friends for company.
I welcome my friends into my home,
but You are my heart's Beloved,
the guest of my soul.

Alone,
I find peace,
for You are always there with me.
Nothing matches Your love.
In all the worlds,
I have found nothing
that gives me more joy than Your love.
You plow the desert sand
within my heart
and plant a garden there.

I would give up everything
I can see and touch,
if I could hold Your love in my palm.

Beloved,
if I come to You because I fear Hell,
I don't deserve You.
If I seek You out
because I long for Heaven,
I'll never find You.
"Spiritual" greed is no better
than "worldly" greed.
Both revolve around my ego.
I need nothing
in this world or the next,
only You.
Hell does not exist
within Your presence.
Heaven is only You.
Give me, Beloved,
the endless light
that streams from Your Face.

I have given a name
to my life's single goal:
Love.

The Beloved asks,
"How long will you keeping pounding on
an open door
begging for someone
to open it?
When will you stop
asking for air to breathe
when it's all around you?"

I am fully qualified, Beloved,
to apply for work as a doorkeeper.
I have years of experience,
for I have learned
that what is inside me, I won't let out,
where it can be destroyed,
and what is outside You, Beloved,
I won't let in.
If an unwanted guest slips in,
I send him right out again.
I am a Doorkeeper of the Heart,
not a lump of helpless clay,
unable to protect Your Presence
within me.

Some people pray to You
because they're afraid of the Fire.
Others pray to You
because they want the Garden.
But I will not pray like this.
I am not afraid of the Fire,
and I do not ask for the Garden.
All I ask is the Essence of You—Your Love;
to return to union with You;
and to become Your Face here on Earth.

Beloved, build in my soul
a temple, a shrine, a mosque, or a church,
somewhere I can kneel to You.
Prayer brings me to an altar
where no walls or names exist.
It leads me to the place
where Love has no boundary lines,
where ecstasy pours into itself,
where wings rise up without a mind or body.
Beloved, build in my soul
a temple, a shrine, a mosque, or a church
that dissolves into nothingness,
that dissolves into You.

"Die before you die,"
said the Prophet Muhammad.
One of our body's most intimate acts
is death.
I know who I will kiss when I have died,
and so I practice dying every day.
I was born when I could
finally love all I once feared,
and so my birth and my death
are the same.

Existence is a sacred place,
and no one lives outside its walls.
God is our Mother,
whose eye is always on us.
Every time we cry,
Light reaches out her arms.
The Beloved says to me,
"There is nothing you experience in this life
that will not lead you closer to Me.
You can go nowhere that will not nourish you.
Anything you encounter, I brought to you.
The world is full of My nutrients."

When Jesus weighs in his scales
the priest and the prostitute,
they are both equally precious.
The Beloved asks me,
"Is your soul's face still so shy
that it won't reveal to you your loveliness?
You joined My community at birth.
Unity will refresh your weary soul,
and Love will open your eyes."

O Beloved, take away the evil thoughts
that mix with my prayer.
If not, then take my prayer as it is,
evil thoughts and all.

4

Love Prayers from
Abu Sa'id ibn
Ab'il Khair

ABU SA'ID IBN AB'IL KHAIR (967–1049 CE), known also as Shaikh Abu Saeed Abil Kheir, referred to himself as "Nobody, Son of Nobody." His life, he said, had disappeared into the Heart of God.

Only when I stop believing
in my ego-self,
will I really come to believe
in You.

I seek You, Beloved,
by loving everyone I meet.
Help me to see only good in them.
May I lift them up
when they are with me
and never pull them down
behind their backs.
Make me like a morning breeze,
sweet and warm.
Make me like the sun,
shining warmth on everyone.

I'm in prison, Beloved.
Show me the way out.
Erase from my mind
all that is not You.

The path of religion
and the path of love
are two different roads,
and only one
leads me to You, Beloved.
Love is a fire
that burns away
both belief and nonbelief.
Those who practice love
know You,
regardless of whether
they practice any religion.

Why should I be proud
of any role I hold, Beloved?
I'm like every other human being:
trapped in a cage of dust and water,
heat and oxygen.
Why should I despair
when all my roles are taken from me?
They were only an illusion.

If I could recite from memory
a thousand scripture verses,
that wouldn't erase my ego-self.
Knowledge of scripture
doesn't prove my worth,
when my ego-love proclaims my heresy.
Each time I bow in prayer,
remind me, Beloved,
to drop the load of ego
I carry on my back.
My ego is the bulky thing
that makes me too fat
to get through the door
into Your bedroom.

Feed my mind with tolerance,
Beloved,
and with compassion.
Simplify my life,
so there's more room in it for love.

The less I brood on all I wish I had,
the more room I'll have
inside my inner self
for You, Beloved.
Remind me that my best words
speak of You.

I pray best
in the middle of the night
when I'm all alone
with You, Beloved.

I've found, Beloved,
that the shortest route to You
is by giving myself away to others.
When I stop being selfish,
when I'm generous
with my time, skills, and possessions,
I find You.

When I'm upset by the wrongs
others have done to me,
help me to find within my heart,
a corner of solitude,
where I forget everything
in the silent joy
of Your Presence.

I drink from the love
You've poured into my inner self,
and I forget all about my ego.
When I look for her again,
she's dancing in the wind.

Sorrow dwells in me today, Beloved.
I'm filled with longing,
I'm almost losing hope,
and then I hear You say,
"The broken ones in this life
are My darlings."
Crush my heart then, Beloved.
Break me.

If I don't let my ego drop,
Beloved,
I'll never know my true worth.
I offer You all I have,
and all I am.
Now that I have nothing,
I am free of pain.
I know this life's joy.

5

Love Prayers from Khajah Abdullah Ansari

KHAJAH ABDULLAH ANSARI of Herat (1006–1088 CE) was a Sufi Muslim who lived in what is today Afghanistan. He was a spiritual master who wrote both poetry and commentaries on the Qu'ran.

I thought I was looking for You everywhere,
but I was only dreaming.
Then I woke up
and found You right beside me!

Where are You, God?
"Right here," You say,
"in the light that shines between friends.
And right there, in the comfort
that comes to travelers
when they are lonely and far from home.
And here, in you, sweetheart,
within your inner self.
I am the life that lives in you."

The world is full of Your words, Beloved,
and You are Your own interpreter.
Protect me from deception.
Bring me into union
with You.

If I had to choose
between my friend and my own heart,
which should I choose, Beloved?
You answer me,
"What good is a heart
if you have no one to give it to?
Choose your friend, sweetheart,
and you will find your heart."

When I'm focused only
on the world I see and touch,
I can no longer see
the world that lasts forever.
Make my vision clear,
Beloved Friend.

I'm so lonely.
I don't know who I am.
I've lost my very self,
and I don't have a clue who You are.
I'm nothing in this world,
and I've made no progress
in the spiritual world.
"Sweetheart," you whisper in my ear,
"I'm right here.
Listen to your breath.
That's Me."

6

Love Prayers
from Sanai

SANAI (1118–1152 CE) was a Persian mystic who lived in what is today Afghanistan. He wrote *The Walled Garden of Truth*, as well as many other shorter poems. His literary and spiritual influence was immense.

I don't need
to look for You everywhere, Beloved.
You're already looking for me.
I just need to let myself be found.

Beloved God,
if You give the tiniest insect its food,
why should I worry?

Lovers aren't afraid to be hurt.
Beloved, make me brave enough
to love.

Wealth comes and goes.
Either way, doesn't really matter,
because I know, Beloved God,
that wealth and love
don't live in the same world.
Since You live within me,
what else do I need?
Why should I ever complain?

I need to say Your name.
I need to wet my lips
and speak the words out loud.
If I can't, then I'm like a wind
blowing nowhere.
When my mouth is filled with You,
I am like the Earth in spring,
awake, alive.
Make my tongue
like the center of a rose,
spilling out sweetness
into the summer air.

When I am filled with You, Beloved,
I am complete.
Within me is an egoless patience,
waiting on the doorstep of my heart,
content to go in or out.
Within me is a silence
that's undisturbed
by the voices of people
passing in the street.

Beloved, You feel
an ant's foot crawling across a leaf
and a pebble shifting in a stream.
You see the worm hidden in the soil.
You know the amoeba and the paramecium,
and You hear their secret songs of praise.
You have given the tiniest creature its food,
and You open to me
the Holy Way.

At Your door, Loved One,
there is no difference
between Muslim and Christian,
virtuous and guilty,
for all are seekers
of You,
the One for whom all hearts yearn.

God says to me,
"Stop building all those traps around yourself.
Burst free like a lion from a cage.
Worship Me as if you could see Me
with your physical eyes.
You are blind to Me,
but I see you.
You have broken faith with Me
and with yourself,
but I still keep faith with you;
I am truer to you
than you are to yourself;
I treasure you more
than you do yourself."

"The way to Me is long,"
says the Divine Lover,
"only because
you keep putting off the journey.
Take one single step—
and you'll be there.
My forgiveness comes so fast,
that it reaches you even before
'I'm sorry' has taken shape
on your lips."

7

Love Prayers from Attar

ATTAR of Nishapur (1145–1221 CE) was a Persian saint and mystic. His best-known work, *Conference of the Birds*, is an allegory of the soul's quest for reunion with God. He wrote that when he sat down to write poetry, more ideas came into his head than he could ever use in his lifetime. Writing love poems to God sometimes put him into a trance state that lasted throughout an entire sleepless night of creative ecstasy.

Remind me,
Beloved One,
that if I refuse to die to myself,
I will never live.
So long as I identity myself
with something or someone,
I will never be free.
I can never learn to live
in the realm of Love,
if I am obsessed with the realm of the ego.

Beloved God,
help me now,
while I still breathe,
to begin to discover
the Mystery of my own self.
If I can't begin to know myself now,
how will I be able to comprehend
the secret of my own existence
when I die?

I'm beginning to understand
that in Your love
I can no longer speak of
"me" and "You."
My self has merged with You.
Within my inner self,
when I pull back the curtain
that hides my deepest being,
I find You, my Friend.

When I wonder
about the mysteries of this world
and the next,
remind me, Beloved,
that the secret of both worlds
is only this:
Love.

In the dead of night,
Beloved God,
I began to cry,
because I finally understood:
the world in which I live
is like a closed coffin.
I have lived my entire
foolish, lonely life
inside this box.
When Death comes at last
to lift the lid,
I'll spread my wings
and fly off into Eternity,
just like a bird.
But Beloved,
help me even now,

while the lid is still tight
on my coffin,
to do all I can
to be growing my feathers
and my wings.

Show me, Eternal Wisdom,
the reality of this world:
absolutely everything
is in Love's marketplace.
All that comes to us,
comes from Love,
and it is ours.
You made all things in Love.
On Love all things depend;
toward Love all things turn.
The Earth, the sun,
the moon, the stars,
have Love as the center
of their orbits.
Love is what we all need.
Your Love makes us all drunk.

Beloved One,
I have chosen only four things to know.
First, I know that I have enough.
You've given me my share,
and now I've stopped trying
to add to my portion.
Second, I know I owe You
a debt that only I can pay.
I pay it with my life, my love.
Third, I know that someone
is always chasing me.
His name is Death.
Since I can never outrun him,
I might as well prepare myself
for our meeting.
Fourth, I know
that You are always
watching me,
so I will never be lost.

8

Love Prayers from Sa'di

SAADI of Shiraz (1215–1292 CE) was born in what is today a part of Iran, but he traveled as far as India, where he learned from Hindu teachers. He taught that no barriers of faith, nation, or any other thing should separate humans, for we are all "the limbs of a single body, all the shimmering essence of God"; what hurts one of us will hurt everyone. *The Rose Garden* and *The Orchard* are some of his most famous works. Sa'di was his pen name.

Remind me, Beloved,
to stop worrying
so much about impressing others.
Whether I'm a failure
or a success,
may my only goal be
to polish the mirror
of my inner self,
so that Your splendor
may be reflected there
like a flame.

How can I ever thank You,
Beloved Friend?
Each and every hair on my body
is a gift from You,
but I'll never be able to count each hair.
Your gifts are so lavish!
You have clothed me in splendor
from the moment I was born,
until the moment of my death.

Wipe the dust from
my heart's mirror,
Loving God.
As I go to work each day,
as I follow my daily routines,
remind me not to rely
on ego-strength.
You, the Hidden One within my heart,
give me all my skill and strength.
When I am successful,
may I not bask in my achievement,
for wins and losses come to everyone,
both streaming from Your grace.
Beloved One,
My very existence comes from You.
The Invisible sustains me
each moment of my life.

9

Love Prayers from Mahmud Shabistari

MAHMUD SHABISTARI (1288–1340 CE), born in what is now modern-day Iran, lived and wrote during the Mongol invasions. Violence and unrest were as present in his land as they are today—and yet his poetry is full of confident love and joy. Because of his gift for expressing the Sufi mystical vision with extraordinary clarity, his *Secret Rose Garden* became one of the most popular works of Persian Sufi poetry.

I'm sweeping
the floor of my heart, Beloved One.
I'm making it ready for You.
And then I'll leave,
so You can come in.
When my ego's not at home,
You have space within me
to display Your loveliness.

I am only the latticework on a lampshade
through which You shine.
There are other lamps,
and other lattices,
but only One Light.

I am a veil, hiding Heaven from Earth.
Each human being wears a different veil,
but lift each veil, and there is only You.
All the differences we thought we saw
are gone.
What is a mosque?
What is a synagogue?
What is a temple?
What is a church?
They are only more veils,
hiding You.

Oh Beloved One, You have made
the entire world as a mirror.
Within each atom You hid a hundred suns.
In each drop of water
flows all the Earth's oceans.
When I look at a speck of dust,
I see a thousand living things.
A gnat and an elephant are siblings.
In each grain of wheat is stored
a hundred harvests.
An entire world exists
in each seed,
and every insect's wing
is a sea of life.
You hid Heaven
in the pupil of my eye.
The core of my being is so small,
but You, Lord of all the worlds,
are living there.

10
Love Prayers from Yunus Emre

YUNUS EMRE (1241–1321 CE) was a Sufi mystic from Turkey. His simple poetic technique skillfully expressed complicated mystical concepts. His influence today is still so great that his face is on the Turkish 200 lira banknote.

I have lived my life in health and joy:
thank You, Bright One.
When I was dry, You watered me.
You loved me, and I grew wings:
thank You, Shining One.
I was a trickle that turned into a river.
I flowed into the sea,
and now my heart has overflowed:
thank You, Loving One.
I was raw and tasteless,
like uncooked dough,
and now, at last,
You've seasoned me with salt
and baked me!

I ask You,
"What is the soul
that lives within my flesh?"
And You answer,
"The power of all Reality."
My mind's thoughts
are only errand boys
for something greater.
I am everything,
and nothing.
And since I am nothing,
why should I care about money?
Money only buys things
that won't last.
Who are You, Beloved?
Who am I?

When I was born, Beloved,
I entered the house of my senses,
and then I saw the whirling skies,
the many-layered Earth,
night and day,
the planets and the stars.
I learned of religion.
I read the scriptures—
the Torah, the Gospel, and the Qu'ran—
but in these holy books
I found nothing greater
than the truth within my own flesh,
the mystery that lies within me,
beyond the seventy thousand veils
within my body.

How can I comprehend You,
Mysterious One?
You were before,
and You are after.
You help those in need,
and yet others go hungry.
You make the ground flat,
and You make mountains
that rise into the sky.
You guide many to You
through faith and religion,
and yet for others,
You are the sacrilege
that lives inside their hearts.
You are the true faith,
and You are no faith.
Your reality is far greater
than my understanding.

If I try to make claims on Your behalf,
I'm being blasphemous.
You are before,
and You are after.

I've fallen in love with You, Beloved,
and now You've stolen me from myself.
You are all I need, all I crave.
Even if I die,
even if there were nothing left of me
but ashes,
I'd sing out from my grave:
You are all I need,
You are all I crave.

11
Love Prayers from Jami

JAMI (1414–1492 CE) is sometimes referred to as Persia's last great mystical poet. He often used passionate earthly love as a metaphor for spiritual love.

Who am I, Beloved?
You answer me:
"A reflection of Eternal Light,"
What then is the world, Beloved?
"A wave on the Everlasting Sea."
Why do I feel
so separate from You, Beloved?
"You are not separate,"
You say to me.
"How can a reflection
be separate from the light?
How can a wave
be separate from the sea?
Reflection and wave
are one with the light
and with the sea."

Beloved,
from each of the world's
subatomic particles
You created countless mirrors,
and each mirror
reflects Your Face.
But reflections are fleeting.
If I want permanence,
I cannot seek to grasp
at a reflection.
I must cling only to You,
the primal Source of all I see.
Why should I tear my soul apart
over something
that is here one moment
and gone the next?
You, Beloved, are the only constant
hidden within
this world's transient beauty.

HAZELNUTS FROM JULIAN OF NORWICH

Meditations on Divine Love

by ELLYN SANNA

"The Spirit showed me a tiny thing, the size of a hazelnut," wrote the fourteenth-century mystic, Julian of Norwich. In Julian's vision, the fragile and insignificant hazelnut contains all of Creation—and yet it endures "because God loves it."

Seven hundred years before Rob Bell wrote Love Wins, Julian had already offered the world a vision of God's all-encompassing love. These prayer-poems, based on *All Shall Be Well: A Modern-Language Version of the Revelation of Julian Norwich*, are an accessible introduction to Julian's joyous theology of love.

THE HEART OF MEDITATION
INTERFLOW:
Thoughts, Prayers, & Meditations

by GEORGE BREED

In this paperback collection of the e-book series titled *Meditations of the Heart*, the author offers bite-size entries into mindfulness and transformation. Each meditation could be used as a vehicle for greater consciousness—or as a prayer leading to deeper awareness of spiritual reality and being. One Amazon reviewer summarized: "Each tiny gem of a meditation holds meaning beyond and beneath the words, and each provides nourishment for the mind and the heart. Concise, simple, but packed with a powerful load of thought-provoking enlightenment, George Breed gives more to us in his meditations with a dozen or so words than most philosophers give in twelve dozen."

SONG OF A CHRISTIAN SUFI
A Spiritual Memoir

by MARIETTA BAHRI DELLA PENNA

This is the story of a woman's spiritual journey: from the restrictions of growing up as Catholic female in the 1950s to her emotional and spiritual liberation as a Sufi—and to her ultimate return to a new understanding of Christianity. Building on the foundations of the Sufi and Christian mystics, Della Penna's memoir is sometimes funny, sometime heartbreaking—and always points toward more universal truths beyond the particularities of an individual life. It will resonate with anyone seeking to find life's deeper meanings. The author's discovery of her own unique "song" is truly a gift to us all!

www.AnamcharaBooks.com

www.ingramcontent.com/pod-product-compliance
Lightning Source LLC
LaVergne TN
LVHW041624060526
838200LV00040B/1432